RISKY BUSINESS

RISKY BUSINESS

The Management of Risk and Uncertainty

by John Adams

Adam Smith Institute

London

1999

Bibliographical information

Published in the UK in 1999 by
ASI (Research) Ltd, 23 Great Smith Street, London SW1P 3BL
www.adamsmith.org.uk

The majority of this report was first published in 1999 as *Cars, Cholera, and Cows* by the CATO Institute, 1000 Massachusetts Avenue NW, Washington, DC 20001.

© John Adams 1999

ISBN: 1-902737-06-7

Printed in the UK by Imediaprint Ltd.

Contents

About the author

John Adams is professor of geography, University College, London, England. He is the author of *Risk* (1995) and "Virtual Risk and the Management of Uncertainty," in the Royal Society's *Science, Policy and Risk* (1997).

Preface

Risk management is a balancing act. We weigh the rewards of risk against potential adverse outcomes. A zero risk life is not on offer. Taking risks leads, by definition, to accidents. It is possible to be too cautious, to have too few accidents. The speculator's slogan – "No risk, no reward" – is true for all of us.

Everyday risks

Risk management involves making choices in the face of uncertainty. Many of these choices involve mundane *directly perceptible* risks. We manage these sorts of risk instinctively and intuitively – we do not do a formal probabilistic risk assessment before crossing the road. Where the risks concerned are voluntary, the invisible hand of Adam Smith appears to be at work – ensuring that the number of accidents we have is optimal. Neither George Mallory nor Ayrton Senna wanted to die in the way they did, but both were determined to be their own risk managers. So, in a less dramatic way, with crossing the road to catch a bus; if we are late and determined not to miss it, we will take greater risks dodging traffic in order to catch it. No one wants an accident, but we all appear determined to be our own risk managers. Attempts by legislators, regulators and safety campaigners to make us safer than we choose to be are routinely frustrated by behaviour that re-establishes the level of risk we choose to take in pursuit of the rewards we seek.

With involuntary risks – imposed risks – there are limits to the efficacy of the invisible hand. There are many residential streets with fast traffic and good accident records – because children are forbidden to cross them, old people are afraid to cross them, and fit adults cross them quickly and carefully. The good accident records are purchased at the cost of community severance – people on one side of the road do not know their neighbours on the other. One person's freedom to drive fast is another person's imposed risk. How the rights of motorists and residents are to be balanced is a matter for political negotiation.

About one third as many children are killed in road accidents in Britain today as in 1922 when there was a nationwide 20 mph speed limit and hardly any traffic – not because the streets are three times safer for children to play in, but because they are perceived by parents to be so dangerous that they do not let their children out anymore. Should children be withdrawn from the threat, or the threat withdrawn from the children? This is a live question in transport policy debates today. Opinion varies about how the balance should be struck.

Not all risks can be seen by the naked eye. The causes of infectious diseases and cancer, for example can usually only be identified with the help of microscopes and scientists, in turn aided by statisticians and epidemiologists. The use that is made of the information that they provide varies. Again we encounter the distinction between voluntary and involuntary risk

Quite convincing information is now available about the harmful effects of smoking, drinking to excess, and the taking of various drugs, yet many people still do these things – strongly suggesting that, for those who indulge, the perceived rewards outweigh the adverse consequences. As with directly perceptible risks, attempts to criminalise voluntary self-risk have a dismal record. The main effect of prohibition, whether of drink or drugs, has been the spawning of criminal empires.

Where science can show conclusively that someone, say a polluting manufacturer, is imposing risks on others, then as with our first category of risk we encounter a problem of defining rights. Does my entitlement to clean air outweigh your right to pollute. One often proposed way of dealing with such risks is to convert them into voluntary risks by the creation of a market. However, market forces cannot help until this issue of rights is settled. If I am entitled to clean air, the price to be negotiated is the amount of compensation that I will accept for your imposition. If you are entitled to pollute, the price to be negotiated is the amount that I would be willing to pay you to stop. These two prices are not the same. A more common way of dealing with such risks is by means of regulatory standards – the equivalent to an agreed speed limit on a residential street. The process of negotiating such standards is frequently complicated by a lack of agreement about the value of the costs and benefits of the polluting activity, and the fact that the beneficiaries and the bearers of the costs are seldom the same people. The process is even more complicated when the risks at issue are *virtual*.

Virtual risks are products of the imagination which work upon the imagination. The less conclusive the science relating to a particular risk, the more liberated are people's imaginations. BSE/CJD, genetically modified foods and mobile phones are topical examples of virtual risks. In the absence of clear and convincing scientific evidence, judgements about these risks will be influenced by people's predispositions to view the evidence in particular ways. This paper presents a four-fold typology of the predispositions commonly encountered in debates about virtual risks:

- *The individualist* is a cheerful optimist, a believer in market forces and prepared to take a gamble, because you are likely to win more than you lose – if you can't prove it's dangerous assume it's safe. Science provides solutions.

- *The egalitarian* is a worried pessimist concerned that Man's impact on Nature and Society will have devastating consequences; he is also much concerned

6

with the *fairness* of outcomes – if you can't prove it's safe assume it's dangerous. Science creates new risks.

- *The hierarchist* is a careful bureaucrat who assumes all risks ought to be managed; he is very uncomfortable in the presence of virtual risk because his managerial style requires reliable information about the probable consequences of regulatory intervention. Science needs regulating.

- *The fatalist* feels powerless in face of the forces of both Nature and Society – the best you can do is buy lottery tickets, and duck if you see something about to hit you.

These predispositions are deeply entrenched and highly resistant to incompatible information, and when there is no trustworthy information they tend to be the principal determinants of what people believe about hypothesised threats. What people believe about virtual risks depends on whom they believe, and whom they believe depends on whom they trust. Recent surveys of trust by both Mori and academics have produced rather disturbing results. Least trusted (by only about 10% of those sampled) were government and big business; most trusted (by over 80% of the sample) were friends and family. Thus the generators and regulators of most big risks, and those with access to the best information about them, are trusted least, and those with access to the least reliable information are trusted most. This provides fertile soil for the hysteria and paranoia that are routinely exploited by the media whenever they discover a new virtual risk

With such risks the balancing act still involves judgements about rewards and potential adverse outcomes, and these judgements will be strongly influenced by whether the risk is seen is as voluntary or imposed. In terms of the above typology the opposition to genetically modified foods can be viewed as an *egalitarian* crusade; its success, in the absence of any uncontested evidence that GM foods have done any harm, can perhaps be explained by the fact that a) few consumers at present, of any predisposition, see any benefit in eating them, and b) the producers' resistance to labelling, thereby denying the consumer choice, has resulted in GM foods being seen as imposed risks – imposed for the benefit of the producer. If a risk, however small or remote, is accompanied by no perceptible rewards a rational risk manager will have no reason to take it. By contrast, the – slightly more convincing, though still inconclusive – evidence of potential harm caused by mobile phones has not perceptibly impeded the impressive growth rate of this form of communication. Here the risks are largely seen as voluntary and for most people the rewards associated with their use appear to justify the risk.

Policy implications

- New-born infants have all their risk-management decisions taken for them by their parents or guardians. The process of development involves a progressive handing over of these responsibilities until the child reaches the

age of responsibility. Whenever the state intervenes to over-ride decisions made by adults about risks to themselves that they freely choose to take, it fairly earns the title "The Nanny State". Attempts to regulate self-risks *voluntarily assumed* will fail, or have perverse effects – Adam Smith's Invisible Hand Rules OK!

- Attempts to regulate *imposed* risks can succeed only to the extent that the regulated – both those constrained and those protected – have good reason to trust the regulator. This, given the conflicting interests and predispositions involved in risk debates, is a tall order. An optimal state of collective self-interest is one that has been defined by economists – they call it Pareto optimality – but not yet achieved in practice. Untrammelled self-interest, where definitions of self-interest rest are rooted in different predispositions, is unlikely to yield results that everyone will recognise as ideal. Here we are in the realm of Adam Smith's *Theory of Moral Sentiments*.

1. Introduction

Every day, in decisions ranging from crossing the street to considering whether a hamburger is safe to eat, every one of us must face and manage a wide variety of risks. Every such decision involves balancing the uncertain rewards of actions against the potential losses. Figure 1 uses the risk "thermostat" as a model of this balancing act.

Figure 1 The Risk "Thermostat"

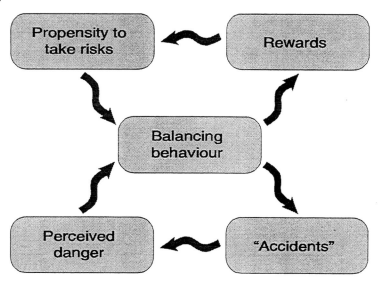

The model postulates that

1.   everyone has a propensity to take risks;

2.   this propensity varies from one individual to another;

3.   this propensity is influenced by the potential rewards of risk taking;

4.   perceptions of risk are influenced by experience of accident losses – one's own and others';

5.   individual risk-taking decisions represent a balancing

6.   act in which perceptions of risk are weighed

7.　against propensity to take risks; and

8.　accident losses are, by definition, a consequence of taking risks; the more risks an individual takes,

the greater, on average, will be both the rewards and the losses he incurs.

There has been a long-running and sometimes acrimonious debate between "hard" scientists – who treat risk as something that can be objectively measured – and social scientists – who argue that risk is culturally constructed. Much of this debate has been caused by the failure of the participants to distinguish among different kinds of risk. It is helpful, when considering how the balancing act in Figure 1 is performed, to be clear about the sort of risk one is dealing with. There are three:

9.　directly perceptible risks, such as climbing a tree, riding a bicycle, and driving a car;

10.　risks perceptible with the help of science, such as cholera and other infectious diseases; and

11.　virtual risks, about which scientists do not or cannot agree, e.g., the connection between bovine spongiform encephalopathy (BSE, or mad cow disease) and CJD (Creutzfeldt-Jakob disease) in humans; global warming; and numerous suspected carcinogens.

In Figure 2 these categories are represented by three overlapping circles to indicate that the boundaries between them are indistinct, and also to indicate the potential complementarity of approaches to risk management that have previously been seen as adversaries in the debate between the "hard" scientists and the cultural constructionists.

Figure 2 Three Types of Risk

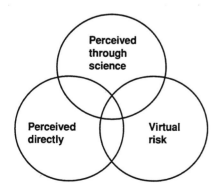

2. Directly perceptible risks

Figure 1 can serve as a description of the behaviour of the driver of a single car going around a bend in the road. His speed will be influenced by his perception of the rewards of risk; these might range from getting to the church on time to impressing his friends with his skill or courage. His speed will also be influenced by his perception of the danger; his fears might range from death, through the cost of repairs and loss of his license, to mere embarrassment. His speed will also depend on his judgment about the road conditions – is there ice or oil on the road? How sharp is the bend and how high the camber? – and the capability of his car – how good are the brakes, suspension, steering, and tires?

Overestimating the capability of the car or the speed at which the bend can be safely negotiated can lead to an accident. Underestimating those things will reduce the rewards gained. The consequences, in either direction, can range from the trivial to the catastrophic. The balancing act described by this illustration is analogous to the behaviour of a thermostatically controlled system. The setting of the thermostat varies from one individual to another, from one group to another, from one culture to another, and for all of these, over time. Some like it hot – a Hell's Angel or a Grand Prix racing driver, for example – others like it cool – a Caspar Milquetoast or a little old lady named Prudence. But no one wants absolute zero.[1]

Risk: An Interactive Phenomenon

Figure 3 introduces a second car to the road to make the point that risk is usually an interactive phenomenon. One person's balancing behaviour has consequences for others. On the road one motorist can impinge on another's "rewards" by getting in his way and slowing him down, or help him by giving way. One is also concerned to avoid hitting other motorists or being hit by them. Driving in traffic involves monitoring the behaviour of other motorists, speculating about their intentions, and estimating the consequences of a misjudgment. Drivers who see a car approaching at high speed and wandering from one side of the road to the other are likely to take evasive action, unless perhaps they place a very high value on their dignity and rights as a road user and fear a loss of esteem if they are seen giving way. During this interaction enormous amounts of information are processed.

Figure 3 The Risk Thermostat: Two Drivers Interacting

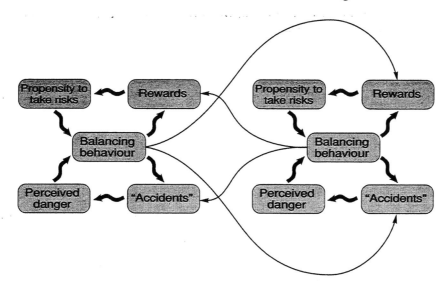

Moment by moment each motorist acts upon information received, thereby creating a new situation to which the other responds.

Figure 4 The Risk Thermostat: Truck Driver and Cyclist Interacting

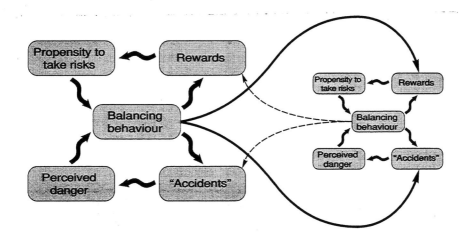

Figure 4 introduces a further complication. On the road and in life generally, risky interaction frequently takes place on terms of gross inequality. The damage that a heavy truck can inflict on a cyclist or pedestrian is great; the physical damage that a cyclist or pedestrian might inflict on the truck is small. The truck driver in this illustration can represent the controllers of large risks of all sorts. Those who make the decisions that determine the safety of consumer goods, working conditions, or large construction projects are, like the truck driver,

12

usually personally well insulated from the consequences of their decisions. The consumers, workers, or users of their constructions, like the cyclist, are in a position to suffer great harm, but not inflict it.

Risk Compensation: The Case of Seat Belt Legislation

The phenomenon illustrated by Figures 1, 3, and 4 is commonly termed "risk compensation"[2] or "offsetting behaviour." As people perceive themselves as safer or better equipped against a danger, they are more likely to take more risks. Although the phenomenon is widely accepted as true, it is almost universally denied in risk regulation. The efficacy of seat belt legislation has become an accepted "fact." Now that seat belt laws have been passed in more than 80 jurisdictions around the world, one would expect the evidence in support of the claims for seat belt legislation to be voluminous, but oddly it has shrunk dramatically. The claims now all rest on the experience of only one country, the United Kingdom.[3]

In 1991, after surveying the global evidence, Leonard Evans of the General Motors Research Laboratory reached the following conclusion about seat belt legislation:

> The highest precision evaluation is for the UK's law, where belt use rose rapidly from 40% to 90% in a large population of affected occupants. The law reduced fatalities to drivers and front-seat passengers by 20%. For smaller use rate increases, and for smaller populations (that is, in nearly all other cases), it is not possible to directly measure fatality changes. They can be reliably estimated using an equation based on the known when-used effectiveness of the belts together with a quantification of *selective recruitment* effect – the tendency of those changing from non-use to use to be safer than average drivers.[4]

In other words, according to Evans, of the more than 80 jurisdictions with seat belt laws, fatality reductions can be measured only in the United Kingdom. In all the other jurisdictions the life-saving benefits were too small to register in the accident statistics.

The claims made for seat belt laws in all other jurisdictions rest on a deduction that assumes there is no risk-compensation effect. There is no basis for that assumption. Indeed, there is a vast amount of evidence of measurable response to interventions that influence the outcomes of other sorts of "crashes" – trapeze artists with safety nets, rock climbers with ropes, and lovers with condoms, to cite three obvious examples. All attempt maneuvers with their safety equipment that they would not attempt without it.

It is not clear why the proponents of seat belt legislation believe that protection in car crashes should be an exception to this well-established principle. In fact,

elsewhere in his book, Evans indicates that potential outcome does influence behaviour.

> All drivers I have questioned admit that they would drive more carefully if their vehicles contained high explosives set to detonate on impact; dramatically increasing the harm from a minor crash can clearly reduce the probability of a minor crash.[5]

Evans's evidence concerning the life-saving benefits of seat belts *if one is in a crash* is not disputed. It's intuitively obvious that a person traveling at high speed inside a hard metal shell will stand a better chance of surviving a crash if he is restrained from rattling about inside, and there's an impressive body of empirical evidence showing that the use of a seat belt improves a car occupant's chances of surviving a crash. Evans has calculated that wearing a belt reduces one's chances of being killed if in a crash by 41 percent. He assumes that this benefit has been enjoyed by all those people in the 80-plus jurisdictions who belted up in response to a law, and the laws therefore can be given credit for saving large numbers of lives. But it does seem curious that with such a large effect, and despite the fact that hundreds of millions of motorists all around the world are now compelled by law to wear seat belts, he has no confidence in the
data to demonstrate directly measurable fatality reductions except in the United Kingdom. Given the significance attached to the United Kingdom result, we look at it more closely.

The UK Seat Belt Law

As a concession to the doubts that had been raised about seat belt efficacy in the early 1980s, Britain's first seat belt law was passed for an unusual three-year trial period. It came into effect in January 1983 but was not made permanent until another vote in Parliament in January 1986. During those three years, the Department of Transport reduced the claim for lives saved from 1,000 a year to 200.[6] The lower figure was described as a "net" reduction; the decrease in the numbers of people killed in the front seats of cars and vans in 1983 was partially offset by an increase in the numbers of pedestrians, cyclists, and rear seat passengers killed.[7] This shift in fatalities was consistent with the risk-compensation hypothesis that predicted that the added sense of security provided by belts would encourage more heedless driving, putting other road users at greater risk. Despite this implicit acknowledgment of risk compensation, the evidence on which Parliament relied when it confirmed the law in 1986 was fundamentally flawed: it ignored the effect of drunken driving.

The number of road accident deaths had been decreasing at a near-steady rate from at least 1971 through 1981. In 1982, however, there was a noticeable increase that was restricted to the hours between 10:00 p.m. and 4:00 a.m., the so-called drunk driving hours. The downward trend in road accident deaths continued at all other hours in 1982.

The 1982 "alcohol blip" occurred almost entirely in non-built up areas, and it has never been satisfactorily explained. In the words of a Transport and Road Research Laboratory Report, "The series for drinking car drivers in non-built up areas shows an increase in 1982 which cannot be related to available explanatory variables."[8]

Just as there was an increase in road accident deaths in 1982, there was a decrease in 1983 after the seat belt law went into effect. Although some experts jumped to the conclusion that the seat belt law accounted for the decrease, that conclusion ignored the effects of the campaign initiated against drunk driving in 1983.

The decrease in fatalities in 1983 was clearly related to the campaign against drunken driving. In that year,

- "evidential" breath testing was introduced;

- unprecedented numbers of breath tests were administered;

- the number of motorists successfully prosecuted for drunken driving increased by 31 percent;

- the decrease in road deaths between 10 at night and 4 in the morning was 23 percent, while in all other hours it was only 3 percent – in line with the prevailing trend; and

- the percentage of dead drivers whose blood alcohol was over the legal limit dropped from 36 percent to 31 percent.

In advocating the retention of the seat belt law in the 1986 parliamentary debate, the Department of Transport relied most heavily on the analysis of two statistics professors, James Durbin and Andrew Harvey from the London School of Economics. The time-series models developed by Durbin and Harvey for their analysis of the seat belt effect were impressively sophisticated, but none contained alcohol-related variables. They attributed all of the decrease in fatalities in 1983 below the projected trend to the beneficial effect of the seat belt law, and none to the campaign against drunken driving. In a presentation to a Royal Statistical Society seminar, Durbin and Harvey acknowledged that their analysis had taken no account of alcohol and said that the effects of alcohol need future research study. But no studies have so far explained why seat belts have been so extraordinarily selective in saving the lives only of those who are over the alcohol limit and driving between 10 at night and 4 in the morning.

In summary, there were two major road-safety measures introduced by the British government in 1983: the seat belt law and the campaign against drinking and driving. In that year, there was a small, temporary drop in road accident fatalities below the established trend. The evidence with respect to seat belts suggests that the law had no effect on total fatalities but was associated with a redistribution of danger from car occupants to pedestrians and cyclists. The

evidence with respect to alcohol suggests that the decrease in fatalities in 1983 during the drink-drive hours is accounted for partly by the still unexplained rise above the trend in 1982 and partly by the drink-drive campaign in 1983.

The evidence from Britain, which has been singled out as the only jurisdiction in the world in which it is possible to measure fatality changes directly attributable to a seat belt law, suggests that the law produced no net saving of lives. It did, however, redistribute the burden of risk from those inside vehicles, who were already the best protected, to those outside vehicles, who were the most vulnerable.

The Management of Directly Perceptible Risks

The management of directly perceptible risks – by toxicologists, doctors, the police, safety officials, and numerous other "authorities" – is made difficult and frustrating by individuals' insisting on being their own risk managers and overriding the judgments of risk experts and the interventions of safety regulators – a phenomenon routinely attested to by millions of smokers, sunbathers, consumers of jelly-filled donuts, and drinking and speeding motorists. Why do so many people insist on taking more risks than safety authorities think they should? It is unlikely that they are unaware of the dangers – there can be few smokers who have not received health warnings, and, indeed, most smokers overestimate their risks. It is more likely that the safety authorities are less appreciative of the rewards of risk taking.

Directly perceptible risks are "managed" instinctively; our ability to cope with them has been built into us by evolution – contemplation of animal behaviour suggests that it has evolved in non-human species as well. Our method of coping is also intuitive; we do not do a formal probabilistic risk assessment before we cross the street. There is now abundant evidence, particularly with respect to directly perceived risks on the road, that risk compensation accompanies the introduction of safety measures that do not reduce people's propensity to take risks. Statistics for death by accident and violence, perhaps the best available aggregate indicator of the way in which societies cope with directly perceived risk, display a stubborn resistance, over many decades, to the efforts of safety regulators to reduce them.[9]

3. Risk perceived through science

The risk and safety literature does not cover all three categories of risk equally. It is overwhelmingly dominated by the second category – risks perceived through science (Figure 5).

Central to this literature is the *rational actor,* a creature from the imaginations of risk experts,[10] who manages risks on the basis of the experts' judgment about how a rational optimizer would, *and should,* act if in possession of all relevant scientific information. In this literature economists and scientists strive together to serve the interests of someone we might call *Homo economicus-scientificus* – the offspring of the ideal economist and the ideal scientist.

Figure 5 The Dominance of the Rational Actor Paradigm in the Risk and Safety Literature

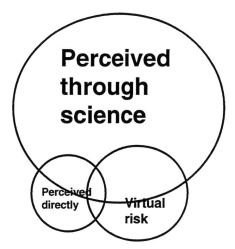

Figure 6 Trends in Mortality: Britain 1841-1980
Source: British Medical Association, *Living with Risk,* 1987.

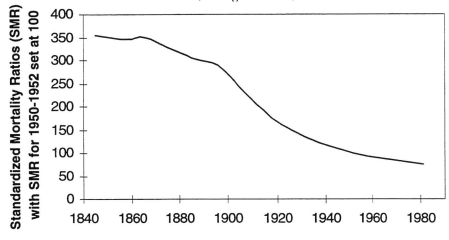

Infectious diseases such as cholera are not directly perceptible. One requires a microscope to see the agents that cause them and scientific training to understand what one is looking at. Science has an impressive record in making invisible or poorly understood dangers perceptible, and in providing guidance about how to avoid them.

Large, and continuing, decreases in premature mortality over the past 150 years, such as those shown for Britain in Figure 6, have been experienced throughout the developed world. Such trends indicate that ignorance is an important cause of death and that science, by reducing ignorance, has saved many lives. When the connection between balancing behaviour and accidents that is shown in Figure 1 is not perceptible, there is no way that knowledge of cause and effect can inform behaviour.

The Institutional Management of Risk

This is the realm of risk quantification. Every individual performs the mental balancing act described in Figure 1 in his or her own head. Institutions – government departments or large commercial enterprises – usually assign the job of risk management to particular people or departments who have no (or very little) balancing responsibility and rarely consider rewards to be gained from particular actions. Individuals confronting directly perceivable risks usually make risk decisions informally and intuitively. Institutions conduct the process explicitly and formally, wherever possible expressing risk in terms of magnitudes and probabilities.

Figure 7 sets out the sequence of steps recommended in a formal risk assessment. Figure 8 describes a similar set of procedures used by a large pharmaceutical company to manage risk.[11] The risk literature is replete with similar algorithms. But, however sophisticated, the shaded overlays that I have added show that when compared with Figure 1 they are simply more elaborate versions of *the bottom loop* of the risk thermostat model. Figures 7 and 8 illuminate the propensity of risk managers to ignore the rewards of risky behaviour and the varying attitudes that individuals take toward risks.

Risk management in institutional settings, with a few exceptions such as insurance and venture capital enterprises, turns out on inspection to be exclusively concerned with *risk reduction*. Institutional risk management models characteristically have no top loop; the "rewards" loop is the responsibility of some other department, often marketing. This view was reinforced during a seminar I presented to the risk managers of a large private-sector concern, when one of the participants said, rather morosely in response to this suggestion, "Yeah, that's right. Around here we're known as the sales prevention department." The following pronouncements from Shell Oil are typical of institutional risk managers whose objective is the elimination of *all* accidents.

The safety challenge we all face can be very easily defined – to eliminate all accidents that cause death, injury, damage to the environment or property. Of course this is easy to state, but very difficult to achieve. Nevertheless, that does not mean that it should not be our aim, or that it is an impossible target to aim for. [12]

The aim of avoiding all accidents is far from being a public relations puff. It is the only responsible policy. Turning "gambling man" into "zero-risk man" (that is, one who manages and controls risks) is just one of the challenges that has to be overcome along the way.[13]

The single-minded pursuit of risk reduction by institutional managers inevitably leaves the pursuers disappointed and frustrated. The risk thermostat model and the evidence supporting it suggest that safety interventions that do not lower the settings of the risk thermostats of the individuals at whom the interventions are aimed are routinely offset by behavioural responses that reassert the levels of risk that people were originally content with. This problem is compounded by the division of labor usually found in institutional risk management; different people or departments are commonly placed in charge of the top and bottom loops with no one obviously in charge of the overall balancing act.

Figure 7 The Risk Assessment Process, Government Style
Source: *A Guide to Risk Assessment and Risk Management for Environmental Protection* (London: Her Majesty's Stationery Office, 1995).

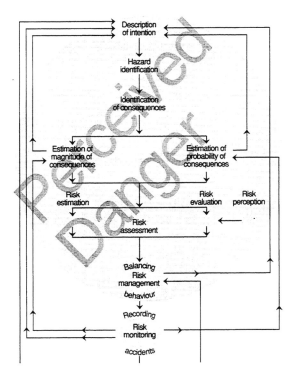

Figure 8 Risk Assessment Process in a Large Pharmaceutical Company

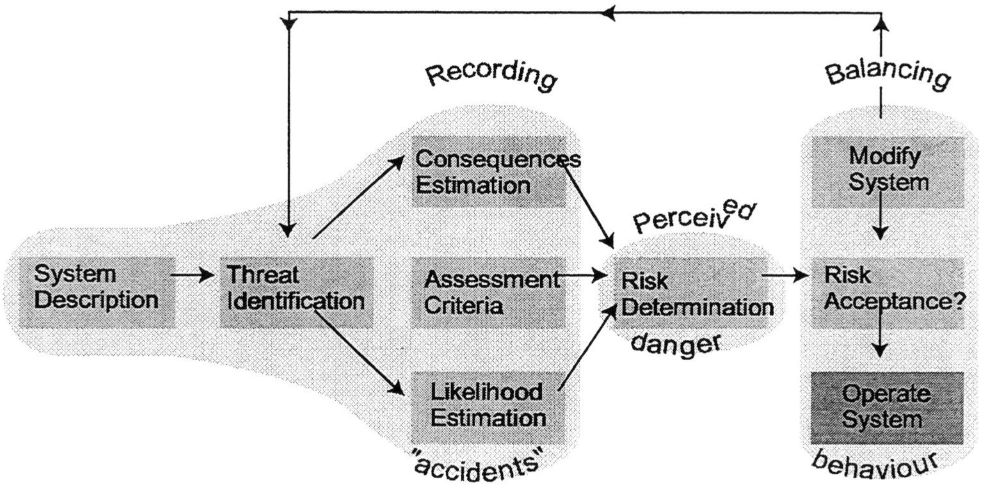

Some Limitations to Scientific Risk Management: A Richter Scale for Risk?

Homo economicus-scientificus is an expert gambler, sensitive to small variations in the odds associated with the risks he runs. The adherents to the rational actor paradigm, the authors of most of the "scientific" risk literature, frequently express their dismay at the inability of ordinary people to make sensible use of such information. As one of their tasks, they seek ways to make laypeople better informed and more "rational" in their risk-taking decisions. Central to the rationalist perspective on risk management is the insistence that all risks can, and should, be reduced to numbers.

In Great Britain the Department of Trade and Industry has proposed the development of a "Richter Scale for Risk" that would "involve taking a series of common situations of varying risk to which people can relate."[14] The Royal Statistical Society has called for "a simple measure of risk that [people] can use as a basis for decision making."[15] The chief medical officer of health has called for the development of an agreed standard scale for communicating information about risk to the general public,[16] and the collection of risks presented in Table 1 is a typical example of what he had in mind.

The risk of dying in a road accident (1:8000) is intended to represent the *average* risk of dying in a road accident; it is derived by dividing the number of people killed in a given year by the total population. It is commonly found about halfway down such tables. It is included because road accidents are the most common cause of accidental death – and hence assumed to be a familiar "benchmark" risk to which people can relate for purposes of seeing other risks in proper perspective. But there are a number of problems with this number that cast doubt on the utility of the table as a guide to individual risk-taking decisions.

Table 1   Risk of an individual's dying (D) in any one year or developing an adverse response (A)

Term Used	Quantitative Risk Range	Example	Measured Risk
High	Greater than 1:100	A. Transmission to susceptible household contacts of measles or chickenpox	1:1-1:2
		A. Transmission of HIV from mother to child (Europe)	1:6
Antibiotics		A. Gastrointestinal effects of	1:10-1:20
Moderate	1:100-1:1000	D. Smoking 10 cigarettes per day	1:200
		D. All natural causes, age 40 years	1:850
Low	1:1000-1:10000	D. All kinds of violence and Poisoning	1:3300
		D. Influenza	1:5000
		D. Accident on road	1:8000
Very low	1:10000-1:100000	D. Leukemia	1:12000
		D. Playing soccer	1:25000
		D. Accident at home	1:26000
		D. Accident at work	1:43000
		D. Homicide	1:100000
Minimal	1:100000-1:1000000	D. Accident on railway	1:500000
		A. Vaccination-associated polio	1:1000000
Negligible	Less than 1:10000000	D. Hit by lightning	1:10000000
		D. Release of radiation by nuclear power station	1:10000000

Source: *On the State of the Public Health: The Annual Report of the Chief Medical Officer of the Department of Health for the Year 1995* (London: Her Majesty's Stationery Office, 1996), p. 13.

First, the number is out of date. The most recent number is 1:15686,[17] about half the number in Table 1, moving road accidents from the "low" to the "very low" category. But this error is trivial compared with the complications that would arise should an individual seek to base a risk-taking decision upon it.

A trawl through the road safety literature[18] reveals that a young man is 100 times more likely to be involved in a severe crash[19] than is a middle-aged woman; someone driving at 3 a.m. Sunday, 134 times more likely to die than someone driving at 10 a.m. Sunday; someone with a personality disorder 10 times more likely to die, and someone at two and a half times the blood alcohol limit 20 times more likely to die. If these factors were all independent of each other, one could predict that a disturbed, drunken young man driving at 3 a.m. Sunday would be about 2.7 million times more likely to be involved in a serious road accident than would a normal, sober, middle-aged woman driving to church seven hours later.[20]

These four factors, of course, are not independent; there are almost certainly proportionately more drunken and disturbed young men on the road in the early hours of the morning than at other times of day. But I have listed only four complicating factors from a very long list.

Does the car have worn brakes, bald tires, a loose suspension, and a valid registration? Is the road well lit, dry, foggy, straight, narrow, clear, congested? Does the driver have good hearing and eyesight, a reliable heart, a clean license? Is the driver sleepy, angry, aggressive, on drugs? All these factors, and many more, can influence a motorist's chances of arriving safely.

A further complication is that the numbers cited above relating to age, sex, time of day, and so forth are themselves averages about which one would expect to find considerable variation. To the extent that the risks of motoring are felt to be directly perceptible, the risk-balancing behaviour of motorists will be guided by their individual perceptions of risk and reward. So whether the number used for road accidents on the Richter Scale is 1:8000 or 1:16000, it is difficult to see how it could serve as a guide to an individual risktaking decision.

Consider another "familiar" risk comparison frequently found in risk tables – the risk of death in an air crash. It is commonly asserted that the fear of flying is irrational, because "objectively" flying is safer than driving. John Durant, in a paper for the Royal Society's Conference on Science, Policy and Risk, sets out what might be called the orthodox-expert view of the safety of flying and the problem created by popular "subjective biases."

The fact that many people behave as if they believe that driving a car is safer than flying in an aeroplane (when on objective criteria the opposite is the case) has been attributed to a combination of the greater dread associated with plane crashes and the greater personal control associated with driving. Faced with a mismatch between scientific and lay assessments of the relative risks of driving and flying, few of us are inclined to credit the lay assessment with any particular validity. On the contrary we are more likely to use the insight to help overcome our own subjective biases in the interests of a more "objective" view.[21]

Evans succinctly deconstructs this view.[22] He begins with the most commonly quoted death rates for flying (0.6/billion miles) and road travel (24/billion miles) and comes to a much less commonly quoted conclusion. He notes

1.   that the airline figure includes only passengers, while the road figure includes pedestrians and cyclists;

2.   that the relevant comparison to make with air travel is the death rate on the rural Interstate system, which is much lower than the rate for the average road;

3.   that the average road accident death rates that lead to the conclusion that it is safer to fly are strongly influenced by the high rates of drunken young

men, while people dying in air crashes are, on average, much older and, when on the road, safer-than-average drivers; and

4.   that because most crashes occur on take-off or landing, the death rate for air travel increases as trip length decreases.

Taking all those factors into account he concludes that a 40-year-old, belted, alcohol-free driver in a large car is slightly less likely to be killed in 600 miles of Interstate driving – the upper limit of the range over which driving is likely to be a realistic alternative to flying – than on a trip of the same distance on a scheduled airline. For a trip of 300 miles he calculates that the air travel fatality risk is about double the risk of driving. This comparison, of course, is not the complete story. The risks associated with flying also should be disaggregated by factors such as aircraft type and age; maintenance; airline; the pilot's age, health, and experience; weather; and air traffic control systems.

Insurance

The insurance industry uses, generally successfully, past accident rates to estimate the probabilities associated with future claim rates. This success is sometimes offered as an argument for using the cost of insuring against a risk as a measure of risk that would be a useful guide to individual risk takers. Weinberg has argued that "the assessment is presumably accurate, since in general it is carried out by people whose livelihood depends on getting their sums right."[23]

However, the fact that the livelihoods of those in the insurance business depend on "getting their sums right" does not ensure that the cost of insuring against a risk provides a good measure of risk *for individuals*. The sum that the insurance business must get right is the *average* risk. For most of the risks listed in Table 1, the variation about the average will range, depending on particular circumstances, over several orders of magnitude. Insurers depend on ignorance of this enormous variability because they need the good risks to subsidize the bad. If the good and bad risks could be accurately identified, the good ones would not consider it worthwhile to buy insurance, and the bad ones would not be able to afford it.

This is precisely the threat to the insurance business posed by discoveries about genetic predisposition to fatal illness. The greater the precision with which individual risks can be specified, the less scope remains for a profitable insurance industry. The current debate about whether insurance companies should be allowed to demand disclosure of the results of genetic tests focuses attention on the threat to the industry of knowledge that assists the disaggregation of these averages. If disclosure is not required, people who are poor risks will be able to exploit the insurance companies; and if it is required, the insurance companies will be able to discriminate more effectively against the bad risks – making them, in many cases, uninsurable.

The companies want access to the results to protect them from exploitation by customers who have access to the information. That knowledge converts risks to certainties (or at least permits risks to be specified more accurately) and reduces the size of their market.

Problems of Measurement

Risk comes in many forms. In addition to economic risks – such as those dealt with by the insurance business – there are physical risks and social risks, and innumerable subdivisions of these categories: political risks, sexual risks, medical risks, career risks, artistic risks, military risks, motoring risks, legal risks. The list is as long as the number of adjectives that might be applied to behaviour in the face of uncertainty. These risks can be combined or traded. People are tempted by the hazard pay available in some occupations. Some people, such as sky-diving librarians, may have very safe occupations and dangerous hobbies. Some young male motorists would appear to prefer to risk their lives rather than their peer-group reputations for courage.

Although the propensity to take risks is widely assumed to vary with circumstances and individuals, there is no way of testing this assumption by direct measurement. There is not even agreement about what units of measurement might be used. Usually the assumption is tested indirectly by reference to accident outcomes; on the basis of their accident records, young men are judged to be risk seeking, and middle-aged women to be risk averse. But this test inevitably gets muddled up with tests of assumptions that accidents are caused by errors in risk perception, which also cannot be measured directly. If Dale Earnhart crashes at 200 mph in his racing car, it is impossible to determine "objectively" whether it was because he made a mistake or because he was taking a risk and was unlucky.

Beyond the realm of purely financial risk, both the rewards of risk and accident losses defy reduction to a common denominator; this renders unworkable the economist's preferred method for performing the risk-management balancing act – cost/benefit analysis. The rewards come in a variety of forms: money, power, glory, love, affection, self-respect, revenge, curiosity satisfied, or simply the sensation (pleasurable for some) accompanying a rush of adrenaline. Nor can accident losses be measured with a single metric. Road accidents, the best documented of all the realms of risk, can result in anything from a bent bumper to death, and there is no formula that can answer the question, How many bent bumpers equal one life? The search for a numerical measure to attach to the harm or loss associated with a particular adverse event encounters the problem that people vary enormously in the importance they attach to similar events. Slipping and falling on the ice is a game for children and an event with potentially fatal consequences for the elderly.

Figure 9 is a distorted version of Figure 1 with some of the boxes displaced along an axis labeled "Subjectivity-Objectivity." The box that is displaced farthest in the direction of objectivity is "balancing behaviour." It is possible to measure behaviour directly. It is, for example, well documented that parents have withdrawn their children from the streets in response to their perception that the streets have become more dangerous.[24] It is possible in principle to measure the decline in the amount of time that children spend in the streets exposed to traffic, but even here the interpretation of the evidence is contentious. Do children now spend less time on the street because they spend more time watching television, or do they spend more time watching television because they are not allowed to play in the streets?[25] All of the elements of the risk-compensation theory, and those of any contenders of which I am aware, fall a long way short of the objective end of the spectrum. Behaviour can be measured, but its causes can only be inferred.

Moreover, risks can be displaced. If motorcycling were to be banned in Britain it would save about 500 lives a year. Or would it? If it could be assumed that all the banned motorcyclists would sit at home drinking tea, one could simply subtract motorcycle accident fatalities from the total annual road accident death toll. But at least some frustrated motorcyclists would buy old clunkers and try to drive them in a way that pumped as much adrenaline as their motorcycling did, and in a way likely to produce more kinetic energy to be dispersed if they crashed. The alternative risk-taking activities that they might pursue range from skydiving to glue sniffing, and there is no set of statistics that could prove that the country had been made safer, or more dangerous, by the ban.

Figure 9 The Risk Thermostat Stretched

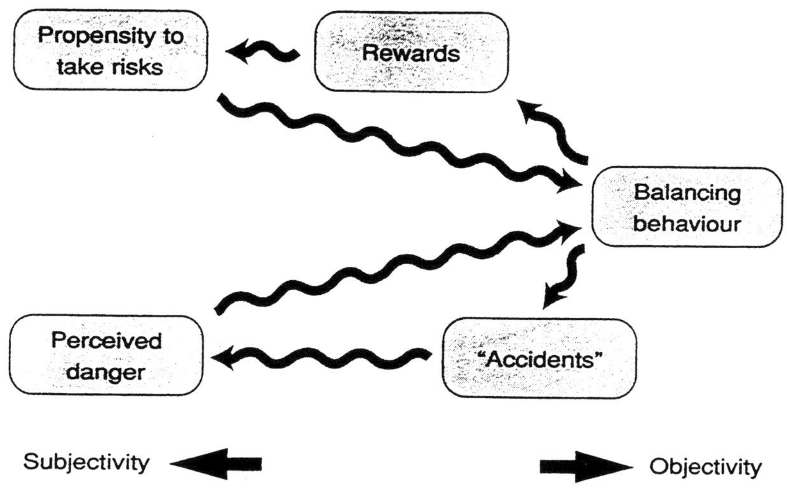

If a road has many accidents it might fairly be called dangerous; but using past accident rates to estimate future risks can be positively misleading. There are many dangerous roads that have good accident records *because* they are seen to be dangerous – children are forbidden to cross them, old people are afraid to

cross them, and fit adults cross them quickly and carefully. The good accident record is purchased at the cost of community severance – with the result that people on one side of a busy road tend no longer to know their neighbors on the other. But the good accident record gets used as a basis for risk management. Officially – "objectively" – roads with good accident records are deemed safe and in need of no measures to calm the traffic.

The Dance of the Risk Thermostats

Figure 10 is an attempt to suggest a few of the complications confronting those who seek objective measures of risk that flow from the reflexive nature of risk. The world contains more than 5.5 billion risk thermostats. Some are large – presidents with fingers on buttons – most are tiny – children chasing balls across streets. Governments and big businesses make decisions that affect millions if not billions of people. Individuals for the most part adapt as best they can to the consequences of those decisions. The damage that they individually can inflict in return, through the ballot box or market, is insignificant, although in aggregate they can become forces to reckon with; the slump in the market for beef in response to fears of BSE has not only caused losses to the beef industry, but set off a Europe-wide political chain reaction. Overhanging everything are the forces of nature, floods, earthquakes, hurricanes, plagues, which even governments cannot control, although they sometimes try to build defenses against them. And fluttering about the dance floor are the Beijing butterflies beloved of chaos theorists: they ensure that the best laid plans of mice and men "gang aft agley." Figure 10 shows but an infinitesimal fraction of the possible interactions between all the world's risk thermostats; there is not the remotest possibility of ever devising a model or building a computer that could predict accurately all the consequences of intervention in this system. The broken line symbolizes the uncertain impact of human behaviour on nature.

Figure 10 The Dance of the Risk Thermostats

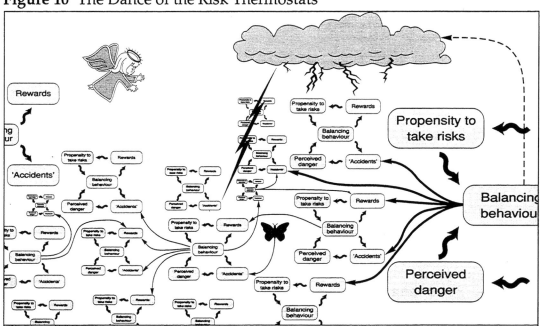

The winged creature at the top left was added in response to a *Time* magazine survey (December 27, 1993) that revealed that 69 percent of Americans believe in angels and 46 percent believe they have their own guardian angel. The "angel factor" must influence many risk-taking decisions – in mysterious ways.

A small part of the dance can be observed directly in crowded local shopping streets on any Saturday morning as cyclists, pedestrians, cars, trucks, and buses all contend for the same road space. But not all the dangers confronting the participants in this dance are visible to the naked eye. Some cyclists can be observed wearing masks to filter the air. Lead, oxides of nitrogen, carbon monoxide, volatile organic compounds, and ultra-fine particulates are all invisible substances that some of the better informed shoppers might worry about. Few of those worried people will be toxicologists capable of judging the dangers directly. Their concerns will usually be based on scientific pronouncements filtered through the media and perhaps augmented by the campaigns of environmentalists.

The dance of the thermostats with its multiple connections can also be viewed as a description of the way in which an infectious disease is passed among risk takers. Infectious diseases are important to the discussion of risks perceived by science because science has an impressive record in reducing dangers from infectious diseases. For example, the insight that cholera is spread through some water supplies led to closing down sources of contaminated water and improved sanitation that controlled the spread of the disease more than 30 years before the responsible bacterium was identified by laboratory scientists.[26] The spread of sanitation efforts, combined with vaccination, has virtually eradicated cholera from the developed world.

The risk thermostat still plays a part in responses to infectious disease risks. Now many tourists, protected by vaccination, venture into parts of the world where they would previously have feared to go – thereby exposing themselves to other diseases and dangers. There are numerous other examples of science's defeating risks only for people to reassert their determination to take risks. The Davy lamp was heralded as a safety device that reduced the danger of explosions in mines because it operated at a temperature below the ignition point of methane. But it permitted the expansion of mining into methane-rich atmospheres and was followed by an increase in mining productivity along with explosions and fatalities in the methane-laden environments. Since improvements in brake technology, when fitted to cars, usually result in drivers' going faster, or braking later, the potential safety benefit gets consumed as a performance benefit.

The Meaning of "Probability"

The probabilities that scientists attach to accidents and illnesses, and to the outcomes of proposed treatments, are quantitative, authoritative, confident-

sounding expressions of uncertainty. They are not the same as the probabilities that can be attached to a throw of a pair of dice. The "odds" cannot be known in the same way, because the outcome is not independent of previous throws. When risks become perceptible, when the odds are publicly quoted, the information is acted upon in ways that alter the odds.

One form that this action might take is new research to produce new information. Britain's chief medical officer of health (Sir Kenneth Calman) says, "It is possible for new research and knowledge to change the level of risk, reducing it or increasing it."[27] This view sits uncomfortably alongside the Royal Society's view[28] of risk as something "actual" and capable of "objective measurement." If risk is "actual" and subject to "objective measurement," how will further research modify it?

This phenomenon might be described as the Heisenberg problem.[29] The purpose of measuring risk is to provide information that can guide behaviour. Statements about risk are statements about the future. Accident statistics, the most commonly used measure of risk, are statements about the past. To the extent that the information conveyed by accident statistics is acted upon, the future will be different from the past. The act of measurement alters that which is being measured.

As scientists, insurance company actuaries, and other risk specialists are successful in identifying and publicizing risks that have previously been shrouded in ignorance, they shift them into the directly perceptible category – and people then act upon this new information. Risk is a continuously reflexive phenomenon; we all, routinely, monitor our environments for signs of safety or danger and modify our behaviour in response to our observations – there-by modifying our environment and provoking further rounds of responses ad infinitum. For example, the more highway engineers signpost dangers such as potholes and bends in the road, the more motorists are likely to take care in the vicinity of the now-perceptible dangers, but also the more likely they are to drive with the expectation that all significant dangers will be signposted.

What Calman perhaps meant when he said that new research might change the level of risk is that the probabilities intended to convey the magnitude of the scientist's uncertainty are themselves uncertain in ways that cannot be expressed as probabilities. He should perhaps have said that a scientific risk estimate is the scientist's "best guess at the time but subject to change in ways that cannot be predicted." This brings us to uncertainty and the cultural construction of risk.

4. Virtual risk

We do not respond blankly to uncertainty; we impose meanings on it. Those meanings are virtual risks. Whenever scientists disagree or confess their ignorance, the lay public is confronted by uncertainty. Virtual risks may or may not be imaginary, but they have real consequences – people act on the meanings that they impose on uncertainty.

The 1995 contraceptive pill scare in Britain is an example of a "scientific" risk assessment spilling over into the virtual category. Britain's Committee on the Safety of Medicines issued a public warning on the basis of preliminary, unpublished, non-peer-reviewed evidence that the new third-generation pill was twice as likely to cause blood clots as the second-generation pill. The result was a panic in which large numbers of women stopped taking the new pill, with the further result that there were an estimated 8,000 extra abortions and an unknown number of unplanned pregnancies. The highly publicized twofold increase in risk amounted to an estimated doubling of fatalities from two to four a year.[30] Even when doubled, the mortality risk was far below that for abortions and pregnancies. Such minuscule risks are statistical speculations and cannot be measured directly. Subsequent research cast doubt on the plausibility of *any additional risk* associated with the new pill. The lesson that the chief medical officer of health drew from this panic (i.e., behavioural response to new information) in his annual report was that "there is an important distinction to be made between relative risk and absolute risk."[31] Just whom he held responsible for the failure to appreciate this distinction – the public or the government's medical experts – he did not make clear.

Perhaps a more important lesson is that scientists, by combining uncertainty with potentially dire consequences, can frighten large numbers of people. Dressing up their uncertainties in very low absolute probabilities does not seem to help – especially when they are presented in a hastily called press conference that begins with the advice "don't panic." Calman observed that "although the increased risk was small, women did need to be informed that there was a difference in risk between the oral contraceptives available to them" and that "the message, to continue to take the oral contraceptive pill, seemed to be ignored in the pressure for action." From where, he might have asked himself, did this pressure for action come? Why, women might sensibly ask themselves, are they giving us this new information with such a sense of urgency if they expect us to take no action?

The women who stopped taking the pill were imposing meaning on the uncertainty of the British medical establishment. This uncertainty was projected through and amplified by the media. The fact of the hastily convened press

conference, the secretive procedures by which the Committee on the Safety of Medicines and other government agencies arrive at their conclusions, and histories of government cover-ups of dangers such as radiation and mad cow disease have resulted in a very low level of public trust in government. A recent British survey that asked people whether they would trust institution X to tell them the truth about risks found that only 7 percent would trust the government, compared to 80 percent who said they would trust environmental organizations.[32] This mistrust feeds a paranoid tendency that can hugely exaggerate trivial dangers.

Cultural Filters

We all, scientists included, perceive virtual risks through different "cultural filters."[33] The discovery of the Antarctic ozone hole was delayed by a physical equivalent of such a filter. U.S. satellites failed to pick up early indications of the hole because programmers had instructed the satellite computers to reject data outside a specified range as errors. As a result, the low readings were trashed as errors.[34]

The influence of filters can also be detected in the debate about the effects of low-level radiation. Despite the accumulation of many decades of evidence, there is still no agreement about whether there is a safe dose, or perhaps even a therapeutic dose. An article in the April 1997 issue of *Chemistry in Britain* states that

> large epidemiological studies for radon levels in parts of the US, Sweden, Finland and China show that the incidence of lung cancer actually decreases with increasing radon exposures, even for levels of up to 300 Bq m -3 . . . even in Cornwall and Devon, where soils and houses contain the highest levels of uranium and radon in the UK . . . the number of lung cancers is lower than in most other regions of the UK – despite the fact that the southwest includes a high proportion of cigarette smokers.[35]

This provoked a strong reply from G. M. Kendall and C. R Muirhead of Britain's National Radiological Protection Board, who insisted that radon caused about 2,000 deaths a year in Britain and suggested that the effect in Devon and Cornwall was probably obscured because low smoking rates there caused lower cancer rates even in the presence of high radon levels. But neither side of the argument presented any statistics on smoking in Devon and Cornwall.

John Graham, vice-president in charge of environment, safety and health for British Nuclear Fuels Inc., takes the argument one step further, advancing the hypothesis that low-level radiation can have beneficial effects.[36] He argues that background radiation routinely causes cell damage, for which effective repair mechanisms exist, and that there are optimum exposure levels at which the stimulation of the repair mechanisms outweighs the damage. This lay spectator judges the debate to be still unresolved.

When scientists do not know or cannot agree about the "reality" of risks, people are liberated to argue from belief and conviction. Thompson, Ellis, and Wildavsky[37] identified four distinctive "rationalities" of belief and conviction through which people view the world and manage their risks. Each of the four rationalities is associated with a "myth of nature," illustrated by the behaviour of a ball in a landscape (Figure 11).

As described in Table 2, individualists see nature as benign (and robust); it can be made to do what humans command. Egalitarians see nature as ephemeral; nature is to be obeyed. Hierachists see nature as alternately perverse and tolerant; with proper attention to rules, nature can be managed. Fatalists see nature as capricious; nature has the upper hand; there's nothing to be done.

Where do average people fall on Figure 11 and Table 2? Depending on context and circumstance, they can find themselves in any or all of the categories.

Figure 11 Four Rationalities: A Typology of Bias
Source: Adams, *Risk.*

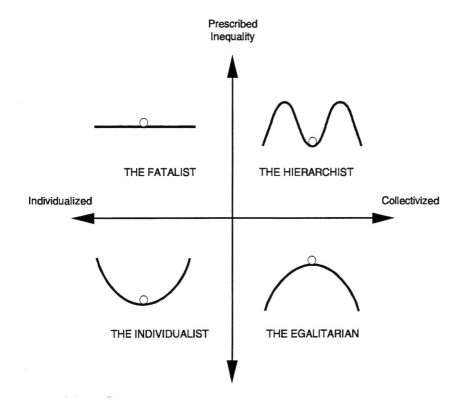

Table 2 Rationalities of belief and their associated myths of nature

Rationality Myth of Nature

• **Individualists: nature benign**

Individualists are enterprising "self-made" people, relatively free from control by others, who strive to exert control over their environment and the people in it. Their success is often measured by wealth and the number of followers they command. The self-made Victorian mill owner and present-day venture capitalist are good representatives of this category. They oppose regulation and favor free markets. Nature is to be commanded for human benefit.

Nature benign is represented by a ball in a cup (see Figure 11): nature, according to this myth, is predictable, bountiful, robust, stable, and forgiving of any insults humankind might inflict upon it; however violently it might be shaken, the ball comes safely to rest in the bottom of the basin. Nature is the benign context of human activity, not something that needs to be managed. The individualist's management style—relaxed, exploitative, laissez-faire—fits this myth.

• **Egalitarians: nature ephemeral**
Egalitarians have strong group loyalties but little respect for externally imposed rules, other than nature's. Their central rule is the precautionary principle, considered necessary to protect nature from human abuses. Group decisions are arrived at democratically and leaders rule by force of personality and persuasion. Members of religious sects, communards, and environmental pressure groups all belong to this category. Nature is to be obeyed.

Nature ephemeral is represented by a ball balanced precariously on an overturned cup: here nature is fragile, precarious, and unforgiving. It is in danger of being provoked by human greed or carelessness into catastrophic collapse. People, the myth insists, must tread lightly on the earth. The egalitarian's guiding management rule is the precautionary principle; it is necessary to obey nature.

• **Hierarchists: nature perverse/tolerant**
Hierarchists inhabit a world with strong group boundaries and binding prescriptions. Social relationships in this world are hierarchical and everyone knows his or her place. Members of castebound Hindu society, soldiers of all ranks, and civil servants are exemplars of this category. Nature is to be managed.

Nature perverse/tolerant combines modified versions of the first two myths. Within limits, nature can be relied upon to behave predictably. It is forgiving of modest shocks and can look after itself in minor matters. Care must be taken not to knock the ball over the rim; regulation is required to prevent major excesses. This is the ecologist's equivalent of a mixed economy model. The hierarchist manager's style is interventionist.

• **Fatalists: nature capricious** Fatalists have minimal control over their own lives. They belong to no groups responsible for the decisions that rule their lives. They are non-unionized employees, outcasts, refugees, untouchables. They are resigned to their fate and see no point in attempting to change it. Nature, they expect, will throw things at them, and the best they can do is duck if they see something coming.

Nature capricious: nature is unpredictable. The appropriate management strategy is laissez-faire, in the sense that there is no point to management. Where adherents to the myth of nature benign trust nature to be kind and generous, the believer in nature capricious is agnostic; the future may turn out well or badly, but in any event, it is beyond his control. The fatalist's non-management motto is que sera sera.

Coping with Risk and Uncertainty: The Dose-Response Curve

Wherever the evidence in a dispute is inconclusive, the scientific vacuum is filled by the assertion of contradictory certitudes. There are numerous risk debates, such as those about the relationship between BSE and CJD, in which scientific certainty is likely to be a rare commodity for the foreseeable future. Issues of health, safety, and the environment – matters of life and death – will continue to be decided in the absence of conclusive scientific knowledge.

32

Just how remote is the prospect of scientific resolution, and how large is the scientific vacuum, can be illustrated with the help of some numbers taken from a report by the U.S. National Research Council,[38] which notes that about 5 million different chemical substances are known to exist and that the risks from every one are theoretically under federal government regulatory jurisdiction. In 1983, when the report was first published, fewer than 30 chemicals had been definitely linked to cancer in humans, and about 7,000 had been tested for carcinogenicity in animals.

Even allowing for the advances of cancer research since 1983, these last two numbers almost certainly greatly exaggerate the extent of existing knowledge. Given the ethical objections to direct testing on humans, tests for carcinogenicity are done on animals. The NRC report observes, "There are no doubt occasions in that observations in animals may be of highly uncertain relevance to humans"; it also notes that the transfer of the results of these tests to humans requires the use of scaling factors that can vary by a factor of 35 depending on the method used and observes that "although some methods for conversion are used more frequently than others, a scientific basis for choosing one over the other is not established."[39] A further difficulty with such experiments is that they use high doses in order to produce results that are clear and statistically significant for the animal populations tested. But for every toxic chemical, the dose levels at issue in environmental controversies are probably much lower.

Figure 12 Alternative Dose-Response Extrapolations from the Same Empirical Evidence

Source: National Research Council, Risk Assessment in the Federal Government, p. 263.

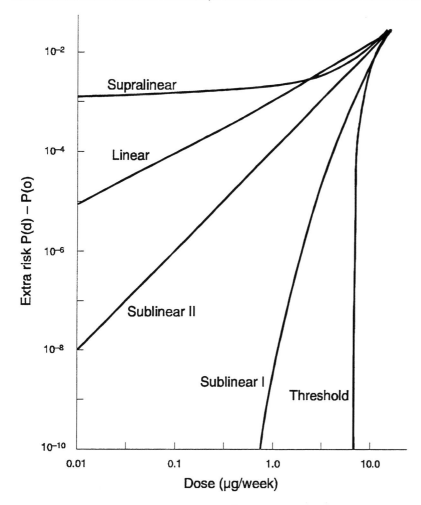

A mathematical model is necessary to extrapolate from the effects at high dose levels at which effects are unambiguous for animals to the much lower exposures experienced by the general human population. Figure 12 illustrates the enormous variety of conclusions that might be drawn from the same experimental data, depending on the assumptions used in extrapolating to lower doses. In many cases, there is only a single data point – almost never more than two – from an animal test. Those points, which are related to numbers of tumors at high doses, anchor all the extrapolation lines so that, as shown on Figure 12, the estimates produced by the five different models are in reasonable agreement in the upper right-hand corner of the graph. The models agree that high dose levels produce high response levels. But the models diverge at lower doses, and at doses that are typical of human exposure levels, the estimates of risk can differ by factors of 10,000 or more. Thus, cultural filters, not science, dictate choices among the models.

- The supralinear model *assumes* that the level of risk will remain high as dose levels are reduced.

- The linear model, preferred by U.S. regulatory agencies for estimating the risks from all carcinogens and by regulatory agencies in other countries for estimating risks from carcinogens that directly affect DNA,[40] *assumes* that there is a direct relationship between dose and risk. Reducing the dose by a factor of two reduces risk by the same amount.

- The two sublinear models *assume* that reducing the dose by a factor of two reduces the risk by a greater factor. Such models are often proposed by regulated industries in the United States, but they have not been adopted by regulatory agencies.

- The threshold model *assumes* that risk falls to zero when the dose levels fall below a certain value, the threshold dose. Threshold models are used by regulatory agencies in European countries to estimate risks for carcinogens that do not directly affect DNA, but they are rarely used in the United States.[41]

Four other sources of uncertainty are of even greater significance in making risk estimates. First, variability in susceptibility within exposed human populations, combined with the variability in their levels of exposure, makes predictions of the health effects of substances at low dose levels a matter of guesswork. Second, the long latency period between exposures to most carcinogens – such as cigarettes and radiation – and the occurrence of cancer makes the identification of many carcinogens and their control impossible before the exposure of the public. Third, the synergistic effects of substances acting in combination can make innocent substances dangerous, and the magnitude of the number of combinations that can be created from 5 million substances defies the capabilities of all known computers. And fourth, the gremlins exposed by chaos theory (represented in Figure 10 by the Beijing butterfly) will always confound the seekers of certainty in complex systems sensitive to initial conditions.

Figure 13 shows the risk thermostat fitted with cultural filters.[42] The mythological figures of cultural theory are caricatures, but they have numerous real life approximations in debates about risk. Long-running controversies about large-scale risks are long running because they are scientifically unresolved and unresolvable within the time scale imposed by the necessity of making decisions. This information void is filled by people who rush in from the four corners of cultural theory's typology asserting their contradictory certitudes. The clamorous debate is characterized not by irrationality but by plural rationalities.

The contending rationalities not only perceive risk and reward differently, but they also differ according to how the balancing act ought to be performed.

• Individualists scorn authority as the "nanny state" and argue that decisions about whether to wear seat belts or eat beef should be left to individuals and settled in the *market*.

• Egalitarians focus on the importance of *trust*; risk management is a consensual activity; consensus building requires openness and transparency.

• Hierarchists are committed to the idea that the management of risk is the job of *authority* – appropriately assisted by expert advisers. They cloak their deliberations in secrecy or technical mumbo-jumbo[43] because the ignorant lay public cannot be relied upon to interpret the evidence correctly or use it responsibly.

• Fatalists take whatever comes along.

Figure 13 The Risk Thermostat Fitted with Cultural Filters

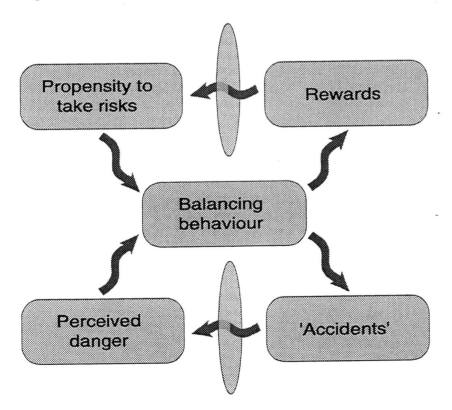

The mad cow disease (or more formally, the bovine spongiform encephalopathy/Creutzfeldt-Jakob disease, BSE/CJD) controversy contains all of the sources of uncertainty discussed with respect to Figure 12. There has been uncertainty and great controversy about whether the "new strain" of CJD that affects young people (called "vCJD" or "variant CJD" to distinguish it from "spCJD" that occurs sporadically in older people) is a human form of BSE. The very existence and nature of prions, the hypothesized agents of transmission of the disease, was hotly disputed,[44] and arguments raged about whether prions are composed only of proteins.[45] Now, however, a scientific consensus is emerging about the causative role of prions in diseases such as BSE and CJD.[46]

Up until now BSE/vCJD research has concentrated on demonstrating the *possibility* of BSE jumping the species divide from cows to humans. Estimation of the *dose levels* at which it becomes a significant threat and identification of the causes of variation in susceptibility are still projects to be worked on. The long and variable latency period for spongiform diseases makes reconstruction of past exposures to presumed causes and exploration of hypotheses about synergistic effects extremely difficult. Great uncertainty surrounds the origins of vCJD, and vCJD remains an extremely rare disease. With all that uncertainty, it's no surprise that people respond differently to the limited information that is available.

Individualists, assiduous collectors of information, are comfortable with uncertainty. Their optimism makes them gamblers – they expect to win more than they lose. Markets in their view are institutions with a record of coping with uncertainty successfully. If the experts cannot agree about BSE, there is no basis upon which central authority can act; the risk should be spread by letting individual shoppers decide for themselves.

The egalitarian instinct in the face of uncertainty is to assume that authority is covering up something dreadful and that untrammeled markets will create something worse. Egalitarians favour democratizing the balancing act by opening up the expert committees to lay participation and holding public inquiries to get at the truth, which they expect will show nature to be precariously balanced on the brink of disaster. In such cases, the precautionary principle must be imposed to protect nature, and the precautionary principle, which calls for no change unless there is no possibility of adverse outcomes from it, justifies the draconian intervention in markets that they favor. While hostile to external regulation, they are happy to impose strict rules of behaviour upon themselves and others to fend off catastrophe.

Ignorance is a challenge to the very idea of authority and expertise. The response of hierarchists is to conceal their doubts and present a confident public face. Confession of ignorance or uncertainty does not come easily to authority. In the face of uncertainty about an issue such as BSE, they seek to reassure.[47] The spectacle of the minister of agriculture, fisheries, and food's forcing his daughter

to eat a hamburger as a public demonstration of his belief in the safety of British beef was followed by the government-forced slaughter of 2 million cows. It is difficult to imagine that the minister was less certain of the safety of his action than the other decision makers were about the risk when they ordered the slaughter.

The fatalists just carry on, drinking beer, reading *USA Today*, and buying lottery tickets. They might accept invitations to buy a rib roast if an individualist offered. The BSE/vCJD affair demonstrates the provisional nature of lay reactions to official information. When the story first broke, sales of beef plummeted. Sales fell even more in Germany, where the German government maintained that there was no BSE, than in Britain. A year and a half later, when the British government banned the sale of beef on the bone as an additional precaution, the newspapers were full of stories of people rushing to purchase the proscribed meat before the ban came into effect.[48] This perhaps demonstrates the difficulty that the news media have in maintaining a state of alarm in the absence of a high body count.

As recently as the summer of 1997 the *British Medical Journal* summed up the state of knowledge thus: "We do not know how or indeed if bovine spongiform encephalopathy is transmitted to humans."[49] One of the report's "key messages" was that "the observation of a group of comparatively young patients with Creutzfeldt-Jakob disease characterized by unusual neuropathological features during 1994-96 remains unexplained."

At that same time, a leading researcher in the field, Professor John Collinge, proclaimed in an interview with the *Times* (of London) medical correspondent (August 7, 1997) that "CJD could become an epidemic of biblical proportions" (this dramatic quotation served as the headline for the article). Professor Collinge went on to say,

> I am now coming round to the view that doctors working in this field have to say what they think, even though this may give rise to anxieties which later turn out to be groundless. . . . We have to face the possibility of a disaster with tens of thousands of cases . . . we just don't know if this will happen, but what is certain is that we cannot afford to wait and see.[50]

Three days later, the *Sunday Telegraph* published a robust *individualist* response by Christopher Booker to Professor Collinge's *egalitarian* call for precautionary action in the face of uncertainty. The response also raised the question of what the nation could afford:

> The efforts of the scientists behind last year's BSE scare to defend their alleged link with "new variant Creutzfeldt Jacob disease" become ever more comical as the epidemic they promised fails to materialize. . . . How much longer should we continue to look for objective guidance on this matter to experts who have invested so much of their own personal reputations in the theory that a link between BSE and new

variant CJD exists? Faced with a bill now rising above £5 billion... how much longer can we afford it?[51]

There has been no epidemic of biblical proportions; there was a total 23 cases of vCJD as of January 1, 1998, in the UK, and no patterns in terms of occupation or eating habits have been found among the 23.[52] The absence of common habits or exposures among the afflicted people weakens any connection that can be drawn between mad cow disease and CJD. But the numbers are very small, the analysis is inconclusive, and there is a possible incubation period of unknown length.

Who knows about the future? A news article in *Nature* neatly captured the "on the one hand, on the other hand" judgment of experts: "The rate of new cases is not increasing . . . but it may be several years before we can be confident that this is not a period of comparative calm before a storm."[53]

Toward the end of 1997 a scientific consensus appeared to be emerging in support of BSE's being the cause of vCJD. But more recently Stanley Pruisner, the winner of the Nobel Prize for his work on prions, pushed the issue firmly back into the realm of virtual risk. The following are excerpts from evidence he presented to the official British government inquiry into BSE on June 6, 1998. (The transcript of his evidence is available at www.bse.org.uk.)

Commenting on the evidence for BSE's causing vCJD he said, "I simply do not understand what all this means. I do not know that this tells us that variant CJD comes from BSE."

What advice could he offer on the safety of beef?

> I have worked in this field for 25 years. And before there was ever BSE I mainly worked on scrapie [a spongiform encephalopathy of sheep], because we did very little on human CJD in the initial phases of the work. Did I go out and eat lamb chops; did I go out and eat lamb brain and sheep brain? The answer was "no," but it was based not on scientific criteria. It was based on just emotion. It is what I said earlier. When there is a disease like BSE things do not sound appetizing. But at a scientific level, I cannot give you a scientific basis for choosing or not choosing beef, because we do not know the answers.[54]

Table 3 BSE/CJD: A Typology of Bias

Fatalist

• "They should shoot the scientists, not cull the calves. Nobody seems to know what is going on." Dairy farmer quoted in the *Times*, August 2, 1996.

• "Charles won't pay for Diana's briefs." Main headline in the Sun on March 21, 1996, the day every other paper led with the BSE story.

Hierarchist

• "We require public policy to be in the hands of elected politicians. Passing responsibility to scientists can only undermine confidence in politics and science." John Durant, *The Times Higher Education Supplement*, April 5, 1996.

• "As much as possible, scientific advice to consumers should be delivered by scientists, not politicians." *The Economist*, March 21, 1996.

• "I believe that British beef is safe. I think it is good for you." Agriculture Minister Douglas Hogg, December 6, 1995.

• "I believe that lamb throughout Europe is wholly safe." Douglas Hogg, July 23, 1996.

• "I felt the need to reassure parents." Derbyshire education chief quoted in the *Sun*, March 21, 1996.

• "I have not got a scientific opinion worth listening to. My job is simply to make certain that the evidence is drawn to the attention of the public and the Government does what we are told is necessary." Health Secretary Stephen Dorrel, *Daily Telegraph*, March 22, 1996.

• "We felt it was a no-goer. MAFF Ministry of Agriculture, Fisheries, and Food, U.K. already thought our proposals were pretty 'radical.'" Richard Southwood, explaining why he had not recommended a ban on cattle offal in human food in 1988. Quoted by B. Wynne, *Times Higher Education Supplement*, April 4, 1996.

Individualist

• "The precautionary principle is favored by environmental extremists and health fanatics. They feed off the lack of scientific evidence and use it to promote fear of the unknown." T. Corcoran, *Toronto Globe and Mail*, March 27, 1996.

• "I want to know, from those more knowledgeable than I, where a steak stands alongside an oyster, a North Sea mackerel, a boiled egg and running for the bus. Is it a chance in a million of catching CJD or a chance in ten million? I am grown up. I can take it on the chin." Simon Jenkins, the *Times*, quoted by J. Durant in *Times Higher Education Supplement*, April 5, 1996.

• "'Possible' should not be changed to 'probable' as has happened in the past." S.H.U. Bowies, FRS, the *Times*, August 12, 1996.

• "It is clear to all of us who believe in the invisible hand of the market place that interference by the calamity-promoting pushers of the precautionary principle is not only hurtful but unnecessary. Cost-conscious non-governmental institutions are to be trusted with the protection of the public interest." P. Sandor, *Toronto Globe and Mail*, March 27, 1996.

• "I shall continue to eat beef. Yum, yum." Boris Johnson, *Weekly Telegraph*, no. 245.

Egalitarian

• Feeding dead sheep to cattle, or dead cattle to sheep, is "unnatural" and "perverted." "The present methods of the agricultural industry are fundamentally unsustainable." "Risk is not actually about probabilities at all. It's all about the trustworthiness of the institutions which are telling us what the risk is." Michael Jacobs, *The Guardian*, July 7, 1996.

• "The Government . . . choose to take advice from a small group of hand-picked experts, particularly from those who think there is no problem." Lucy Hodges, *Times Higher Education Supplement*, April 5, 1996.

• "It is the full story of the beginnings of an apocalyptic phenomenon: a deadly disease that has already devastated the national cattle herd . . . could in time prove to be the most insidious and lethal contagion since the Black Death." The "British Government has at all stages concealed facts and corrupted evidence on mad cow disease."

• "Great epidemics are warning signs, symptoms of disease in society itself." G. Cannon in the foreword to *Mad Cow Disease* by Richard Lacey.

• "My view is that if, and I stress if, it turns out that BSE can be transmitted to man and cause a CJD-like illness, then it would be far better to have been wise and taken precautions than to have not." Richard Lacey, ibid.

Table 3, arranged in the same fashion as Figure 11, presents a representative selection of comments about BSE categorized by cultural theory typology.

- The individualist will continue to believe his risks are small and manageable and want to be left alone with the information that he has or wants.

- The egalitarian will press for more intensive surveillance, more oversight and public participation, and, perhaps, more regulations to guard against the potential "storm."

- The hierarchist may suffer the most; the falling out between political and scientific authority manifest in the upper right-hand corner of Figure 1 is characteristic of the disarray into which hierarchy falls when its mask of authoritative knowledge is torn off – the ball in the top right-hand corner has gone over the rim. He will reassure the public, while commissioning further research as a precautionary measure.

- The fatalist will be the least concerned, perhaps, because he washed his hands of the whole affair a long time ago, if he noticed it at all. Or because he reads the Sun.

5. Should we follow a risk-averse environmental policy?

Who are "we"? "Risk-averse" and "risk-seeking" are usually labels that people apply to others whose risk thermostats are fitted with different cultural filters. Those who argue for a more risk-averse policy are, in effect, saying that there is a discrepancy between the dangers that they perceive and the risks that they are prepared to take. The activities of environmental groups (egalitarians) lobbying for the precautionary principle can be seen as a collective behavioural response to this discrepancy.

The environmentalist case rests on the conviction that growth processes – economic and demographic – are pressing against global limits. Perhaps the best exemplars of this conviction are the Club of Rome authors who argue in *Beyond the Limits* that

> the human world is beyond its limits. The future, to be viable at all, must be one of drawing back, easing down, healing... The more we compiled the numbers, the more they gave us that message, loud and clear. [55]

In the BSE debate the complementary message that is received and retransmitted loud and clear by egalitarians is that BSE is a punishment for unnatural methods of agriculture. Modern intensive, high-energy production methods, veal crates, battery chickens, genetic manipulation, food preservation methods, pesticides, and feeding meat to herbivores are all, according to this perspective, aspects of the same hubristic syndrome. The remedy? Nature is to be obeyed; we must (re)turn to more humane and extensive, organic, *natural* methods of production.

This message is countered by an individualist backlash that views the environmental lobby itself as an environmental threat. Julian Simon, for example, insists that there is a positive correlation between indices of material wealth and an *improving* environment. With Herman Kahn, he has argued,

> We are confident that the nature of the physical world permits continued improvement in humankind's economic lot... indefinitely... There are always newly arising local problems, shortages, and pollutions... But the nature of the world's physical conditions and the resilience in a well-functioning economic and social system enable us to overcome such problems, and the solutions usually leave us better off than if the problem had never arisen; that is the great lesson to be learned from human history.[56]

41

This "rationality," when confronted with the evidence of BSE/CJD, sees no evidence of serious harm. It points to the enormous benefits of intensive agricultural production: the freedom from toil and drudgery provided by modern machinery, the improved nutrition and material standards of living enjoyed by both farmers and consumers, the vast range of choice now available to food shoppers. Their version of the precautionary principle sees all these benefits being placed in jeopardy by an overreaction to tenuous scientific evidence about the cause of a very rare illness.

One side, embracing the precautionary principle, says that if you cannot prove it is safe, you must treat it as dangerous. The other side, citing examples such as the fact that aspirin would never have gotten onto the market if all its real and potential side effects had been known, says that such an approach would quickly bankrupt any endeavor and argues that if you cannot prove it is dangerous, you should treat it as safe.

Governments, the hierarchists, are caught in the middle. Committed to the idea that problems such as BSE can be managed and embarrassed by their manifest failure to do so convincingly, they sought to reassure the public that eating British beef was *probably* safe and commissioned more research that they hoped would confirm it. When it didn't, they initiated a program of mass slaughter, which they justified, not on the grounds that it was necessary to contain the disease, but on the grounds that it was necessary to restore public confidence.[57]

Finally the fatalist, unless he was one of the 23 to fall victim to vCJD or knows someone who did, might know nothing about BSE-vCJD. Noticing that some cuts of beef are missing from the butcher shop, he might ask and find out that nothing much has happened. Perhaps buttressed in his belief that the whole risk debate is baloney, he might buy a lamb chop.

6. Conclusion

Science has been very effective in reducing uncertainty but much less effective in managing it. The scientific risk literature has little to say about virtual risks – and where the scientist has insufficient information even to quote odds, the optimizing models of the economist are of little use. A scientist's "don't know" is the verbal equivalent of a Rorschach inkblot: some will hear a cheerful reassuring message; others will listen to the same words and hear the threat of catastrophe.

Science has a very useful role in illuminating dangers that were previously invisible, and thereby shifting their management into the directly perceptible category. Where science has been successful, it has reduced uncertainty, and thereby shrunk the domain of risk perceived through science; now that its causes are well understood, cholera, for example, is rarely discussed in terms of risk. But where the evidence is simply inconclusive and scientists cannot agree about its significance, we all, scientists included, are in the realm of virtual risk, in the realm of hypothesis.

Figure 14 indicates the relative significance that I suggest hypotheses should be accorded in risk debates. The future is uncertain. What we do not know about it greatly exceeds what it is ever likely to tell us.

The role of science in debates about risk is firmly established; clearly we need more information and understanding, of the sort that only science can provide, about the probable consequences of "balancing behaviours" for both "rewards" and "accidents." But equally clearly we must devise ways of proceeding in the absence of scientific certainty about such consequences – science will never have all the answers – and in so doing we must acknowledge the scientific elusiveness of risk. The clouds do not respond to what the weather forecasters say about them. People do respond to information about risks, and thereby change them.

Figure 14 Reality?

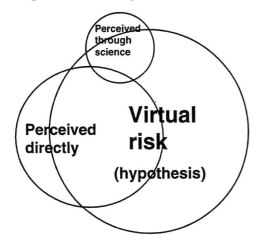

43

In the presence of virtual risk, the precautionary principle becomes an unreliable guide to action. Consider the ultimate virtual risk, discussed from time to time on television and in our newspapers. Edward Teller invoked the precautionary principle to argue for the commitment of vast resources to the development of more powerful H-bombs and delivery systems to enable the world to fend off asteroids – even if the odds of their ever being needed are only one in a million.[58] But we are also told by Russia's defense minister that "Russia might soon reach the thresh-old beyond which its rockets and nuclear systems cannot be controlled."[59] Which poses the greater danger to life on earth – asteroids or H-bombs and delivery systems out of control?

Simon, after a robust display of optimism, observes that nothing has reduced the "doomsayers' credibility with the press, or their command over the funding resources of the federal government."[60] Health and environment debates have a durable and predictable character. The specific issues may change, but the same caricatures from the cultural theory typology reappear in each new debate. The BSE/CJD controversy is but the most recent installment in a much larger, long-running debate. On all sides convictions appear to be as strongly held as ever, and as resistant as ever to contrary evidence.

Scientists have cultural filters about the risks they understand as well as the risks they are trying to understand. For scientists and lay people alike, our cultural filters are parts of our identities and essential to our sense of social solidarity. The persistence of contradictory rationalities built upon partial knowledge suggests that we are doomed, for the foreseeable future, to continue to argue from different premises.

Debates about BSE/CJD, radiation, and asteroid defenses are debates about the future, which does not exist except in our imaginations. They are debates to which scientists have much to contribute, but not ones that can be left to scientists alone. An understanding of the different ways in which people tend to respond to uncertainty cannot settle arguments; but the arguments are likely to be more civilized, and our cultural filters less crudely selective, to the extent that we are sensitive to these differences and understand their causes and effects.

In brief, it is important to be clear about the nature of the risk under discussion. We live in an uncertain world, but certain conclusions about the management of risk might, nevertheless, still be ventured.

Where risks are directly perceptible,

- everyone takes risks; everyone is a risk manager;

- taking risks leads, by definition, to accidents; the pursuit of a world free of accidents is a futile exercise;

- it is important to distinguish self-risk (e.g., driving without a seat belt) from behaviour that puts others at risk (e.g., driving at 100 mph down a busy shopping street); the second is a legitimate area for regulation; the first is not;

44

- attempts to criminalize self-risk are likely to be worse than useless; they are likely to redistribute the burden of risk in ways that harm innocent third parties;

- everyone has a risk thermostat, and he may adjust it so that he has the risk level he likes regardless of the experts' best efforts to decrease risk;

- institutional risk managers who do not take account of the reasons that people have for taking and balancing risks – the rewards of risk – will be frustrated.

Where risks are perceived with the help of science,

- science can reduce uncertainty by illuminating the connection between behaviour and consequence;

- science, effectively communicated, can defeat superstition and purely imaginary scares; but

- science cannot provide "objective" measures of risk;

- risks come in many incommensurable forms that defy reduction to a common denominator;

- the act of measurement alters that which is being measured;

- risk is a reflexive phenomenon; in managing risks we are continually modifying them; in the realm of risk a Heisenberg principle probably rules.

Where scientists don't know or cannot agree,

- we are in the realm of *virtual* risk where plural rationalities contend;

- virtual risks are cultural constructs;

- they may or may not be real – science cannot settle the issue – but they have real consequences;

- the precautionary principle is of no help; different rationalities adhere to very different versions of the principle;

- virtual risks are a fact of life; science will never have all the answers;

- humility in the face of ignorance is a precondition for civilized debate about virtual risks.

Footnotes

1. As discussed below, however, regulators and other institutional managers of risk often proclaim zero risk to be their goal.

2. A term coined by Gerald Wilde in "The Risk Compensation Theory of Accident Causation and Its Practical Consequences for Accident Prevention," Paper presented in 1976 to the annual meeting of the Österreichische Gesellschaft für Unfallchirurgie, Salzburg. His most recent book on this theme is *Target Risk* (Toronto: PDE Publications, 1994).

3. Calls by Cato staff to the National Highway Traffic Safety Administration to obtain research results about how many lives have been saved through seat belt use were unsuccessful.

4. Leonard Evans, *Traffic Safety and the Driver* (New York: Van Nostrand Rheinhold, 1991), p. 278. The evidence concerning the "when-used effectiveness of belts" is based on crash testing using dummies and on paired-comparison studies, which examine the injuries suffered in crashes when one occupant is belted and another unbelted. "Selective recruitment effects" must be allowed for because the timid and cautious are most likely to belt up voluntarily, while the wild and reckless are most likely to defy a law.

5. Ibid., p. 327.

6. Department of Transport, Press release, October 15, 1985.

7. See John Adams, *Risk* (London: Taylor and Francis, 1995), chapter 7.

8. 8J. Broughton and D. C. Stark, *The Effect of the 1983 Changes to the Law Relating to Drink/Driving* (Crowthorne, U.K.: Transport and Road Research Laboratory, 1986).

9. See Adams, *Risk*, chapters 4 and 8, for a discussion of this phenomenon.

10. See Ortwin Renn et al., "The Rational Action Paradigm in Risk Theories: Analysis and Critique," in *Risk in the Modern Age: Science, Trust, and Society*, ed. Maurice J. Cohen (London: Macmillan, 1998, in press).

11. Britain's National Health Service has produced something similar in *Risk Management in the NHS*, Department of Health, July 1996.

12. Richard Charlton, director of exploration and production, Shell Oil, "Where the Buck Stops," *Shell World*, February 1991, p. 8.

13. Koos Visser, head of health, safety, and environment, Shell Oil, "Prudence and the Gambler," *Shell World*, February 1991, pp. 24-25.

14. Minister Ian Taylor in DTI, Press notice P96/686, September 11, 1996.

15. Editorial in *RSS News* 24, no. 4 (December 1996): 1.

16. *On the State of the Public Health: The Annual Report of the Chief Medical Officer of the Department of Health for the Year 1995* (London: Her Majesty's Stationery Office, 1996).

17. *Road Accident Statistics: Great Britain 1995* (London: Her Majesty's Stationery Office, 1996).

18. These factors are taken from U.S. statistics in Evans.

19. Defined by Evans as a crash "of sufficient severity to kill 80-year-old male drivers" (p. 34).

20. Evans, pp. 36, 91, 146; and John Adams, *Risk and Freedom: The Record of Road Safety Legislation* (London: Transport Publishing Projects, 1985), p. 6.

21. John Durant, "Overcoming the Fear of Flying with Joe-Public as Co-Pilot," *Times Higher Education Supplement*, March 14, 1997. "Us" in the context refers, I presume, to his scientific audience at the Royal Society, not the lay public.

22. Evans, p. 362, contains a summary of the argument set out in L. Evans, M. C. Frick, and R. C. Schwing, "Is It Safer to Fly or Drive? – A Problem in Risk Communication," *Risk Analysis* 10 (1990): 259-68.

23. F. Weinberg, Letter to *Times* (London), December 28, 1996.

24. In Britain in 1971, 80 percent of 7- and 8-year-old children got to school unaccompanied by an adult; by 1990 this number had fallen to 9 percent, with parents giving fear of traffic as the principal reason for curbing their children's freedom. M. Hillman, J. Adams, and J. Whitelegg, *One False Move: A Study of Children's Independent Mobility* (London: Policy Studies Institute, 1990).

25. In Britain in the late 1980s, the Department of Transport distributed a leaflet ("A Lesson for Life: Teaching Road Safety for Parents of 1-15 Year Olds") in primary schools, advising parents that it would irresponsible to allow any child under the age of 12 out of the house unaccompanied by an adult.

26. Dr. John Snow mapped the new cases of cholera in an outbreak in London in 1849. The focus of the cluster was the Broad Street well in Soho. The pump handle was removed and the outbreak subsided.

27. *On the State of the Public Health*, p. 8.

28. Royal Society, *Risk: Analysis, Perception and Management* (London: Royal Society, 1992), p. 1.

29. According to Heisenberg's uncertainty principle, the attempt to measure the location of a particle alters its position in an unpredictable way.

30. Quoted on "Anxiety Attack," BBC2, June 11, 1997.

31. *On the State of the Public Health,* p. 9.

32. C. Marris, I. Langford, and T. O'Riordan, "Integrating Sociological and Psychological Approaches to Public Perceptions of Environmental Risks: Detailed Results from a Questionnaire Survey," CSERGE Working Paper GEC 96-07, University of East Anglia, 1996.

33. See Adams, *Risk,* chapter 3, "Patterns in Uncertainty."

34. R. E. Benedick, *Ozone Diplomacy* (Cambridge, Mass.: Harvard University Press, 1991), p. 19.

35. Eric Hamilton, "Radon," *Chemistry in Britain,* April 1997, p. 49. (300 Bq m -3 is equivalent to about twice the Environmental Protection Agency's "level of concern" for radon in homes.)

36. See Bernard L. Cohen, "Lung Cancer Rate vs. Mean Radon Level in U.S. Counties of Various Characteristics," *Health Physics* 72 (1997): 114-19, for an example of an analysis that supports the idea that certain, low levels of radon exposure have beneficial health effects.

37. Michael Thompson, R. Ellis, and A. Wildavsky, *Cultural Theory* (Boulder, Colo.: Westview, 1990).

38. National Research Council, *Risk Assessment in the Federal Government: Managing the Process* (1983; Washington: National Academy Press, 1992).

39. Ibid., p. 27. Since the NRC report was published, the EPA and the FDA, which most depend on animal tests to justify their regulations, have reconciled their differences about scaling factors. They took an average of their competing values. See Environmental Protection Agency, "A Cross-Species Scaling Factor for Carcinogen Risk Assessments Based on Equivalence of mg/kg 3/4 /day," *Federal Register* 57 (1992): 24152-73.

40. See Michael Gough, "Science Policy Choices and Estimation of Cancer Risk Associated with TCDD," *Risk Analysis* 8 (1988): 337-42.

41. Michael Gough and Stephen Milloy, "EPA's Cancer Risk Guidelines: Guidance to Nowhere," Cato Policy Analysis no. 263, November 12, 1996, p. 25.

42. The method of presenting information in Figure 12 might be considered both as the product of a cultural filter and as a cultural filter in its own right. On such a graph it is not possible to show beneficial effects, only harmful effects approaching zero. Why, one wonders, when virtually all of the therapies produced by the pharmaceutical industry, including aspirin, are toxic above certain doses and beneficial below certain doses, should the conventional dose-response curve preclude the possibility of a benign effect? The answer, perhaps, lies in the division of labor discussed above in the section on institutional management of risk. The responsibility of most risk managers is to focus on the bottom loop of Figure 1, to try to minimize the number and magnitude of adverse outcomes. Thus the first question that the U.S. Food and Drug Administration or the British Committee on the Safety of Medicines will ask of a new food or drug is whether it has harmful effects. The emphasis of the manufacturers, the food and drug companies, is likely to be on the top loop, the rewards to the customer and the profits to themselves. For medical risks there is a dearth of risk management institutions that seek to strike a balance between potential adverse and beneficial consequences.

43. Wendy E. Wagner, "The Science Charade in Toxic Risk Regulation," *Columbia Law Review* 95 (1995): 1613-1723.

44. Robert Rohwer, quoted in "Nobody Has Proven That These Prions Really Exist," Special News Report, Science, December 7, 1996. "The prion hypothesis is the 'cold fusion' of infectious disease – it's a very radical idea, and just like cold fusion it has some very appealing aspects. But because it's so radical it deserves a very high level of scepticism and scrutiny before it's adopted."

45. "Not the Last Word on the BSE Crisis," editorial, *Nature* 389 (October 2, 1997): 423

46. Jeffrey Almond and John Pattison, "'Protein Only' Prions," *Nature* 389 (October 2, 1997): 438. For a popular account of the controversy, see Richard Rhodes, "Pathological Science," *New Yorker*, December 1, 1997, pp. 34-49.

47. The propensity of authority to cope with ignorance by denying its existence is described by Jerome Ravetz in "The Sin of Science: Ignorance of Ignorance," *Knowledge* 15, no. 2 (1993): 157-65.

48. Simon Jenkins in *Times* (London), December 6, 1997.

49. S. N. Cousens et al., "Sporadic Creutzfeldt-Jakob Disease in the United Kingdom: Analysis of Epidemiological Surveillance Data for 1970-96," *British Medical Journal* 315 (1997): 389-95.

50. John Collinge, "CJD Could Become an Epidemic of Biblical Proportions," *Times* (London), August 7, 1997.

51. Christopher Booker in *Sunday Telegraph*, August 10, 1997.

52. The National CJD Surveillance Unit, "Sixth Annual Report 1997: Creutzfeldt-Jakob Disease Surveillance in the UK," http://www.cjd.ed.ac.uk/report97.html.

53. Almond and Pattison, p. 438.

54. From http://www.bse.org.uk.

55. D. H. Meadows, D. L. Meadows, and J. Randers, *Beyond the Limits: Global Collapse or a Sustainable Future* (London: Earthscan, 1992), p. xv.

56. Julian Simon and Herman Kahn, eds., *The Resourceful Earth* (Oxford: Blackwell, 1984), p. 3.

57. Martin Woollacott, "Risky Business, Safety" in *The Politics of Risk Society, ed. Jane Franklin* (Malden, Mass.: Blackwell, 1998), chapter 5.

58. Interview on "Big Science," conducted by David Malone, BBC2, August 22, 1995.

59. Quoted in the *Times* (London), February 8, 1997.

60. Julian Simon, *The Ultimate Resource 2* (Princeton, N.J.: Princeton University Press, 1996), p. 15.